HEALING YOUR GRIEVING HEART

Also by Alan Wolfelt:

Creating Meaningful Funeral Ceremonies:
A Guide for Families

Healing a Child's Grieving Heart:
100 Practical Ideas for Families, Friends
and Caregivers

Healing a Friend's Grieving Heart:
100 Practical Ideas for Helping Someone
You Love Through Loss

Healing a Parent's Grieving Heart:
100 Practical Ideas After Your Child Dies

Healing a Teen's Grieving Heart:
100 Practical Ideas for Families, Friends
and Caregivers

Healing Your Grieving Heart for Kids:
100 Practical Ideas

The Journey Through Grief:
Reflections on Healing

Understanding Grief: Helping Yourself Heal

Companion Press is dedicated to the education and support of both the bereaved and bereavement caregivers.

We believe that those who companion the bereaved by walking with them as they journey in grief have a wondrous opportunity: to help others embrace and grow through grief—and to lead fuller, more deeply-lived lives themselves because of this important work.

Companion
P R E S S

For a complete catalog and
ordering information, write or call:

Companion Press
The Center for Loss and Life Transition
3735 Broken Bow Road
Fort Collins, CO 80526
(970) 226-6050
www.centerforloss.com

HEALING YOUR GRIEVING HEART:

•

100 PRACTICAL IDEAS

•

ALAN D. WOLFELT, PH.D.

Companion
PRESS

Fort Collins, Colorado
An imprint of the Center for Loss and Life Transition

Companion Press is an imprint of the
Center for Loss and Life Transition,
3735 Broken Bow Road, Fort Collins, Colorado 80526

Companion Press books may be purchased in bulk for sales
promotions, premiums or fundraisers. Please contact the
publisher at the above address for more information.

Printed in the United States of America

11 09 08 07 06 05 04 03 02   5 4 3 2

ISBN: 1-879651-25-4

*To the thousands of people
in my 25 years of caregiving who have allowed me
the privilege of companioning them in grief.
You have enriched my life,
my living and my loving.
Thank you.*

*I wonder why love is so often equated with joy
when it is everything else as well. Devastation, balm,
obsession, granting and receiving excessive value, and
losing it again. It is recognition, often of what you are
not but might be. It sears and it heals. It is beyond pity
and above law. It can seem like truth.*

Florida Scott-Maxwell
The Measure of My Days

INTRODUCTION

Someone you have given love to and received love from has died. You are in mourning. You are bereft. To be "bereaved" literally means "to be torn apart" and "to have special needs." I am truly sorry for your loss.

Perhaps your most important "special need" right now is to be compassionate with yourself. The word compassion literally means "with passion." So, self-compassion means caring for oneself "with passion." While I hope you have excellent outside support, this little book is intended to help you be kind to yourself. Over my years of walking with people in grief, I have discovered that many of us are hard on ourselves when we are in mourning. We often have inappropriate expectations of how "well" we should be doing with our grief.

These expectations result from common societal messages that tell us to be strong in the face of grief. We are told to "carry on," to "keep your chin up," and to "keep busy." In actuality, when we are in grief we need to slow down, to turn inward, to embrace our feelings of loss and to seek and accept support. It's not easy to be self-compassionate in our mourning-avoiding culture.

But good self-care is essential to your survival. To practice good self-care doesn't mean you are feeling sorry for yourself; rather, it means you are allowing yourself to heal. For it is in nurturing ourselves, in allowing ourselves the time and loving attention we need to journey through our grief, that we find meaning in our continued living. It is in having the courage to care for our own needs that we discover a fullness to living and loving again.

As promised, this book contains 100 practical ideas to help you practice self-compassion. Some of the ideas will teach you about the principles of grief and mourning. One of the most important ways to help yourself is to learn about the grief experience; the more you know, the less likely you will be to unknowingly perpetuate some of our society's harmful myths about grief and healing.

The remainder of the 100 ideas offer practical, here-and-now, action-oriented tips for embracing your grief. Each idea is followed by a brief explanation of how and why the idea might help you.

You'll also notice that each of the 100 ideas suggests a "carpe diem," which means, as fans of the movie *Dead Poets Society* will remember, "seize the day." My hope is that you will not relegate this book to your shelves but keep it handy on your nightstand or desk. Pick it up often and turn to any page; the carpe diem suggestion will help you seize the day by helping you move toward healing today, right now, right this minute. If you come to an idea that doesn't seem to fit you, ignore it and flip to a different page.

I hope that the 100 practical self-care ideas and principles in this resource encourage you to nurture yourself in ways that bring hope and healing.

Alan D. Wolfelt

1.

UNDERSTAND THE DIFFERENCE BETWEEN GRIEF AND MOURNING.

- Grief is the constellation of internal thoughts and feelings we have when someone loved dies.

- Mourning is the outward expression of grief.

- Everyone who has the capacity to give and receive love grieves when someone loved dies, but if we are to heal, we must also mourn.

- Many of the ideas in this book are intended to help you mourn this death, to express your grief outside of yourself. Over time and with the support of others, to mourn is to heal.

CARPE DIEM:
Ask yourself this: Have I been
mourning this death or have I restricted myself to grieving?

2.

BE COMPASSIONATE
WITH YOURSELF.

- The journey through grief is a long and difficult one. It is also a journey for which there is no preparation.

- Be compassionate with yourself as you encounter painful thoughts and feelings of loss and grief.

- Don't judge yourself or try to set a particular course for healing.

- Let your journey be what it is. And let yourself—your new, grieving self—be who you are.

CARPE DIEM:

Look at yourself in the mirror and say, "I am in mourning. I will be compassionate with myself as I mourn this death in my own unique way and in my own time."

3.

UNDERSTAND THE SIX NEEDS OF MOURNING

Need #1: Acknowledge the reality of the death.

- You must gently confront the difficult reality that someone you loved is dead and will never physically be present to you again.

- Whether the death was sudden or anticipated, acknowledging the full reality of the loss may occur over weeks and months.

- You will first acknowledge the reality of the loss with your head. Only over time will you come to acknowledge it with your heart.

- At times you may push away the reality of the death. This is normal. You will come to integrate the reality in doses as you are ready.

CARPE DIEM:
Tell someone about the death today.
Talking about it will help you work on this important need.

4.

UNDERSTAND THE SIX NEEDS OF MOURNING

Need #2: Embrace the pain of the loss.

- This need requires that we embrace the pain of our loss—something we naturally don't want to do.

- It is easier to avoid, repress or push away the pain of grief than it is to confront it.

- It is in embracing your grief, however, that you will learn to reconcile yourself to it.

- You will probably need to "dose" yourself in embracing your pain. If you were to allow in all the pain at once, you could not survive.

CARPE DIEM:
Reach out to someone who doesn't try to take your pain and sense of loss away. Spend some time with him.

5.

UNDERSTAND THE SIX NEEDS OF MOURNING

Need #3: Remember the person who died.

- When someone loved dies, that person lives on in us through memory.

- To heal, you need to actively remember the person who died and commemorate the life that was lived.

- Never let anyone take your memories away in a misguided attempt to save you from pain. It's good for you to continue to display photos of the person who died. Although it's not always possible or appropriate, it's also good for you to stay in the house you shared with the person who died.

- Remembering the past makes hoping for the future possible.

CARPE DIEM:

Brainstorm a list of characteristics or memories of the person who died. Write as fast as you can for 10 minutes (or more), then put away your list for later reflection.

6.

UNDERSTAND THE SIX NEEDS OF MOURNING

Need #4: Develop a new self-identity

- Part of your self-identity was formed by the relationship you had with the person who died.

- You may have gone from being a "wife" to a "widow" or from a "parent" to a "bereaved parent." The way you defined yourself and the way society defines you has changed.

- You need to re-anchor yourself, to reconstruct your self-identity. This is arduous and painful work.

- Many of us find that as we work on this need, we ultimately discover some positive changes, such as becoming more caring or less judgmental.

CARPE DIEM:
Write out a response to this prompt::
I used to be _____. Now that _____ died, I am _____. This makes me feel _____.
Keep writing as long as you want.

7.

UNDERSTAND THE SIX NEEDS OF MOURNING

Need #5: Search for meaning.

• When someone loved dies, we naturally question the meaning and purpose of life and death.

• "Why?" questions may surface uncontrollably and often precede "How" questions. "Why did this happen?" comes before "How will I go on living?"

• You will probably question your philosophy of life and explore religious and spiritual values as you work on this need.

• Remember that having faith or spirituality does not negate your need to mourn. "Blessed are those who mourn for they shall be comforted."

CARPE DIEM:
Write down a list of "why" questions that have surfaced for you since the death. Find a friend or counselor who will explore these questions with you without thinking she has to give you answers.

8.

UNDERSTAND THE SIX NEEDS OF MOURNING

Need #6: Receive ongoing support from others.

- As mourners, we need the love and understanding of others if we are to heal.

- Don't feel ashamed by your dependence on others right now. Instead, revel in the knowledge that others care about you.

- Unfortunately, our society places too much value on "carrying on" and "doing well" after a death. So, many of us are abandoned by our friends and family soon after the death.

- Grief is a process, not an event, and you will need the continued support of your friends and family for weeks, months and years.

CARPE DIEM:
Sometimes your friends want to support you but don't know how. Ask. Call your closest friend right now and tell her you need her help through the coming weeks and months.

9.

ALLOW FOR NUMBNESS.

- Feelings of shock, numbness and disbelief are nature's way of temporarily protecting us from the full reality of the death of someone loved. They help us survive our early grief.

- We often think, "I will wake up and this will not have happened." Mourning can feel like being in a dream.

- Your emotions need time to catch up with what your mind has been told.

- Even after you have moved beyond these initial feelings, don't be surprised if they re-emerge. Birthdays, holidays and anniversaries often trigger these normal and necessary feelings.

CARPE DIEM:
If you're feeling numb, cancel any commitments
that require concentration and decision-making.
Allow yourself time to regroup.

10.

PLAN OR PARTICIPATE IN A MEANINGFUL CEREMONY FOR THE PERSON WHO DIED.

- Rituals are symbolic activities that help us, together with our families and friends, express our deepest thoughts and feelings about life's most important events.

- The funeral ritual is a public, traditional and symbolic means of expressing our beliefs, thoughts and feelings about the death of someone loved.

- Funerals help us:
  - acknowledge the reality of the death.
  - give testimony to the life of the deceased.
  - express our grief.
  - provide support to mourners.
  - embrace our faith and beliefs about life and death.

- Memorial services and other remembrance ceremonies long after the event of the death are also healing rituals.

CARPE DIEM:
Invite others who loved the person who died to help you plan a personalized, inclusive, meaningful ceremony.

11.

BE AWARE THAT YOUR GRIEF AFFECTS YOUR BODY, HEART, SOCIAL SELF AND SPIRIT.

- Grief is physically demanding. The body responds to the stress of the encounter and the immune system can weaken. You may be more susceptible to illness and physical discomforts. You may also feel lethargic or highly fatigued.

- The emotional toll of grief is complex and painful. We often feel many different feelings, and those feelings can shift and blur over time.

- Bereavement naturally results in social discomfort. Friends and family often withdraw from mourners, leaving us isolated and unsupported.

- We often ask ourselves, "Why go on living?" "Will my life have meaning now?" "Where is God in this?" Spiritual questions such as these are natural and necessary but also draining.

CARPE DIEM:

No doubt you are physically impacted by your grief. Make an appointment to see a doctor this week. Sometimes it's comforting to receive a clean bill of health.

12.

USE THE NAME OF
THE PERSON WHO DIED.

- When you're talking about the death or about your life in general, don't avoid using the name of the person who died.

- Using the name lets others know they can use it, too.

- Acknowledge the significance of the death by talking about the person who died: "I remember when David . . .", "I was thinking of Sarah today because . . ."

- Encourage your friends and family to use the name of the person who died, too. We often love to hear that special name.

CARPE DIEM:
Flip through a baby name book at a local bookstore or library and look up the name of the person who died. Reflect on the name's meaning as it relates to the unique person you loved.

13.

CRY.

- Tears are a natural cleansing and healing mechanism. It's OK to cry. In fact, it's good to cry when you feel like it. What's more, tears are a form of mourning. They are sacred!

- On the other hand, don't feel bad if you aren't crying a lot. Not everyone is a crier.

- You may find that those around you are uncomfortable with your tears. As a society, we're often not so good at witnessing others in pain.

- Explain to your friends and family that you need to cry right now and that they can help by allowing you to.

- You may find yourself crying at unexpected times or places. If you need to, excuse yourself and retreat to somewhere private.

CARPE DIEM:
If you feel like it, have a good cry today. Find a safe place to embrace your pain and cry as long and as hard as you want to.

14.

REACH OUT AND TOUCH.

- For many people, physical contact with another human being is healing. It has been recognized since ancient times as having transformative, healing powers.

- Have you hugged anyone lately? Held someone's hand? Put your arm around another human being?

- You probably know several people who enjoy hugging or physical touching. If you're comfortable with their touch, encourage it in the weeks and months to come.

- Hug someone you feel safe with. Kiss your children or a friend's baby. Walk arm in arm with a neighbor.

CARPE DIEM:
Try hugging your close friends and family members today, even if you usually don't. You might find it comforting.

15.

WRITE A LETTER.

- Sometimes articulating our thoughts and feelings in letter form helps us understand them better.

- Write a letter to the person who died telling her how you feel now that she's gone. Consider the following prompts:
  - What I miss most about you is . . .
  - What I wish I'd said or hadn't said is . . .
  - What's hardest for me now is . . .
  - What I'd like to ask you is . . .
  - I'm keeping my memories of you alive by . . .

- Read your letter aloud at the cemetery.

- Write a letter to God telling him how you feel about the death.

- Write notes of appreciation to helpers such as hospice staff, neighbors, doctors, funeral directors, etc.

CARPE DIEM:
Write a letter to someone you love who's still alive,
telling her why she's so important to you.

16.

CREATE A SANCTUARY JUST FOR YOU.

- Mourners need safe places—sanctuaries—where we can go when we feel ready to embrace our grief.

- Create a sanctuary in your own home, a retreat that's just for you.

- Furnish it with a comfy chair, reading materials, a journal, a stereo with appropriate CDs or cassettes. No TV.

- An outside "room" can be equally effective. Do you have a porch or patio where you can just "be"? Locate a comfortable chair and install a table-top fountain.

CARPE DIEM:
Identify a spot in your house that can be your sanctuary. Begin readying it today.

17.

EXPRESS YOUR FAITH.

- Above all, mourning is a spiritual journey of the heart and soul.

- If you have faith or spirituality, express it in ways that seem appropriate to you.

- Attending a church, synagogue, temple or other place of worship, reading religious texts and praying are a few conventional ways of expressing your faith.

- Be open to less conventional ways, as well, such as meditating or spending time alone in nature.

CARPE DIEM:

Visit your place of worship today, either for services or for an informal time of prayer and solitude.

18.

EXPECT TO HAVE A MULTITUDE OF FEELINGS.

- When in grief, we don't just feel sad. We may feel numb, angry, guilty, afraid, confused or even relieved. Sometimes these feelings follow each other within a short period of time or they may occur simultaneously.

- As strange as some of these emotions may seem to you, they are normal and healthy.

- Allow yourself to feel whatever it is you are feeling without judging yourself.

- Talk about your feelings with someone who cares and can supportively listen.

CARPE DIEM:

Using old magazines, clip images that capture the many feelings you've been having since the death. Make a "feelings collage" on poster board and display it somewhere you'll be able to reflect on it often.

19.

KEEP A JOURNAL.

- If you like to write out your thoughts and feelings, journaling is an excellent avenue for self-care.

- Remember—your inner thoughts and feelings of grief need to be expressed outwardly (which includes writing) if you are to heal.

- Consider jotting down your thoughts and feelings each night before you go to sleep. Your journal entries can be as long or as short as you want.

- Or keep a dream journal, instead. Keep a blank book in your nightstand for recording your dreams when you wake up.

CARPE DIEM:

Stop by your local bookstore and choose a blank book you like the look and feel of. Visit a coffee shop on your way home and write your first entry while enjoying a beverage.

20.

TAKE GOOD CARE OF YOURSELF.

- Good self-care is nurturing and necessary for mourners, yet it's something many of us completely overlook.

- Try very hard to eat well and get adequate rest.

- Exercise not only provides you with more energy, it can give you focused thinking time. Take a 20 minute walk every day. But don't over-exercise, because your body needs extra rest, as well.

- Now more than ever, you need to allow time for you.

CARPE DIEM:
Are you taking a multi-vitamin? If not, now is
probably a good time to start.

21.

EAT COMFORT FOOD.

- Comfort food is food that makes you feel safe, loved, at home; it's often associated with foods we ate as children.

- What foods make you feel this way?

- Some examples: mashed potatoes, chicken soup, hot cocoa laden with tiny marshmallows.

- A caveat: Some mourners overeat in an unhealthy attempt to comfort themselves. Strive to eat nutritious foods in reasonable portions.

CARPE DIEM:
Eat something today that brings back pleasant memories of your childhood.

22.

DRINK LOTS OF WATER.

- Grief sometimes overrides our thirst mechanism.

- Dehydration can compound feelings of fatigue and disorientation.

- Drink 4-5 glasses of water each day. Each morning, fill an appropriate-sized pitcher with water and place it in your refrigerator. Add lemon slices if you like. Make it a point to drink the entire pitcher by dinnertime.

- Try teas, sparkling water, juices. Avoid alcoholic and caffeinated beverages.

CARPE DIEM:
Right now, fill an 8-ounce glass with cold water and drink it without setting the glass down.

23.

SLEEP TIGHT.

- Mourning is fatiguing work. Feelings of exhaustion and low energy are extremely common.

- Your body is telling you it needs rest, so indulge your fatigue. Schedule at least 8 hours of slumber into your day. Develop a relaxing bedtime routine so you're ready for sleep.

- Buy yourself new bedding and a good new pillow.

- Lie down for short rest periods periodically throughout the day. Take an afternoon nap if you feel like it.

CARPE DIEM:

Tonight, begin getting ready for bed right after dinner. Take your phone off the hook, bathe or shower, listen to soothing music, sip hot herbal tea in bed as you read a good book.

24.

GO BUY THE BOOK.

- You'll find many good books on mourning and grief at local bookstores and libraries.

- Workbooks (journals, written exercises) can be especially helpful for those who like to put their thoughts and feelings on paper.

- Poetry, religious texts, even novels about loss may be appropriate for some.

- A warning: if you are very fresh in your grief, you may not be ready for so much information or introspection.

CARPE DIEM:
Call Companion Press (970/226-6050) and order a copy of
The Journey Through Grief: Reflections on Healing.

25.

PET A PET.

- Pets are a comforting, loving part of many people's lives. Their physical presence and unconditional love can be healing for mourners.

- Do you have a pet? If so, spend some time caring for your pet today. Buy the pet a new toy or clean its living area.

- If you don't have a pet, would you like one? Keep in mind that pets are a lot of work; especially early in grief, most mourners don't have the energy to care for a new pet. But do consider visiting a pet store or your area animal shelter.

CARPE DIEM:
Buy a book on your favorite animal or pet and
brush up on your knowledge.

26.

CLEAN OUT YOUR CLOSETS.

- The journey through grief can be emotionally chaotic.

- Sometimes amid this chaos it helps to bring order to other aspects of our lives.

- Tackle the messiest closet in your house. Take every single thing out and sort the items in four boxes: Keep. Donate. Trash. Can't Decide.

- Put only the keepers back in the closet.

CARPE DIEM:
Clean out your medicine cabinet. Throw away any outdated medicine, particularly prescription drugs.

27.

UNDERSTAND THE ROLE OF "LINKING OBJECTS."

- You may be comforted by physical objects associated with the person who died. It is not unusual for us to save clothing, jewelry, toys, locks of hair and other personal items.

- Such "linking objects" may help you remember the person who died and honor the life that was lived. Such objects may help you heal.

- Never think that being attached to these objects is morbid or wrong.

- Never hurry into disposing of the personal effects of the person who died. You may want to leave personal items untouched for months or sometimes years. This is OK as long as the objects offer comfort and don't inhibit healing.

CARPE DIEM:
When and only when you're ready, ask a friend or family member to help you sort through the personal effects of the person who died. Fill a memory box with significant objects and mementos.

28.

SIMPLIFY YOUR LIFE.

- Many of us today are taking stock of what's really important in our lives and trying to discard the rest.

- During grief we are often overwhelmed by all the tasks and commitments we have.

- If you can rid yourself of some of those extraneous burdens, you'll have more time for mourning and healing.

- What is it that is overburdening you right now? Have your name taken off junk mail lists, ignore your dirty house, stop attending any optional meetings you don't look forward to.

CARPE DIEM:

Cancel your newspaper subscription(s) if you're depressed by what you read. Quit watching TV news for a while.

29.

TAKE YOUR PHONE
OFF THE HOOK.

- In our hectic lives, the phone is both a can't-live-without-it convenience and an annoying interruption.

- Sometimes we use the phone when we should be talking face-to-face.

- Next time you have an urge to call a friend, drop by and visit him instead.

- Notice how much more intimate and healing it can be to converse in person.

CARPE DIEM:

Take your phone off the hook tonight (or turn the ringer off).
Don't review your messages until tomorrow.

30.

REACH OUT TO OTHERS
FOR HELP.

- Perhaps the most compassionate thing you can do for yourself at this difficult time is to reach out for help from others.

- Think of it this way: Grieving may be the hardest work you have ever done. And hard work is less burdensome when others lend a hand. Life's greatest challenges— getting through school, raising children, pursuing a career—are in many ways team efforts. So it should be with mourning.

- Sharing your pain with others won't make it disappear, but it will, over time, make it more bearable.

- Reaching out for help also connects you to other people and strengthens the bonds of love that make life seem worth living again.

CARPE DIEM:
Call a close friend who may have distanced himself from you since the death and tell him how much you need him right now. Suggest specific ways he can help.

31.

FIND A GRIEF "BUDDY."

- Though no one else will grieve this death just like you, there are often many others who have had similar experiences.

- Find a grief "buddy"—someone who is also in mourning, someone you can talk to, someone who also needs a companion in grief right now

- Make a pact with your grief buddy to call each other whenever one of you needs to talk. Promise to listen without judgment. Commit to spending time together.

- You might arrange to meet once a week for breakfast or lunch with your grief buddy.

CARPE DIEM:
Do you know someone who also needs grief support right now? Call her and ask her out to lunch today. If it feels right, discuss the possibility of being grief buddies.

32.

IGNORE HURTFUL ADVICE.

- Sometimes well-meaning but misinformed friends will hurt you unknowingly with their words.

- You may be told:
  - I know how you feel.
  - Get on with your life.
  - Keep your chin up.
  - This is a blessing.
  - You still (can) have other children.
  - Think of all you have to be thankful for.
  - Now you have an angel in heaven.
  - Time heals all wounds.
  - You're strong. You'll get over it.

- Don't take this advice to heart. Such clichés are often offered because people don't know what else to say. The problem is, phrases like these diminish your unique and significant loss.

CARPE DIEM:
Commit this retort to memory and use it the next time someone tries to comfort you with clichés: "I'm sure you are trying to be helpful, but I don't find your words supportive because_____."

33.

REMEMBER OTHERS WHO HAD A SPECIAL RELATIONSHIP WITH THE PERSON WHO DIED.

- At times your appropriately inward focus will make you feel alone in your grief.

- Think about others who were affected by this death: friends, lovers, teachers, neighbors.

- Is there someone outside of the accepted "circle of mourners" who may be struggling with this death?

- Perhaps you could call her and offer your condolences.

CARPE DIEM:

Today, write and mail a brief supportive note to
someone else affected by the death.

34.

LOOK INTO SUPPORT GROUPS.

- Grief support groups are a healing, safe place for many of us to express our thoughts and feelings.

- Sharing similar experiences with other people experiencing grief may help you feel like you're not alone, that you're not going crazy.

- Your local hospice or funeral home may offer a free or low-cost support group.

- If you are newly bereaved, you may not feel ready for a support group. Often mourners are more open to joining a support group 6-9 months after the death.

CARPE DIEM:
Call around today for support group information. If you're feeling ready, plan to attend a meeting this week or next.

35.

TALK TO A COUNSELOR.

- While grief counseling is not for everyone, many individuals are helped through their grief journeys by a compassionate counselor.

- If possible, find a counselor with experience dealing with issues of grief and loss.

- Ask your friends for referrals to a counselor they've been helped by.

- If you attend a church, your pastor may also be a good person to talk to during this time, but only if he affirms your need to mourn this death and search for meaning.

CARPE DIEM:
Schedule an initial interview with at least two counselors so you can see whom you're most comfortable with.

36.

DO SOMETHING YOU'RE GOOD AT.

- Have other people told you you're good at this or that? Next time you're complimented in this way, take it to heart!

- Often it helps those of us in grief to affirm our worth to others and to ourselves.

- Ride a bike. Bake a cake. Do the crossword puzzle. Write a poem. Play with your kids. Talk to a friend.

- Be on the lookout for talents or gifts that you may possess but never discovered in yourself.

CARPE DIEM:

Make a list of five things you're good at. Do one of them today and afterwards, reflect on how you feel.

37.

BE SILLY.

- At times the seriousness of grief will weigh you down.

- Break free and give yourself permission to do something silly.

- Walk backwards down the sidewalk. Or skip. Or walk on your hands.

- Other ideas: Silly Putty, Groucho Marx glasses, Twister, making faces.

CARPE DIEM:
Kids love being silly. Make up a crazy story and tell it to a 5-year-old today.

38.

TAKE A MINI-VACATION.

- Don't have time to take time off? Plan several mini-vacations this month instead.

- What creative ideas can you come up with to renew yourself? Here are a few ideas to get you started.
  - Schedule a massage with a professional massage therapist.
  - Have a spiritual growth weekend. Retreat into nature. Plan some alone time.
  - Go for a drive with no particular destination in mind. Explore the countryside, slow down and observe what you see.
  - Treat yourself to a night in a hotel or bed and breakfast.
  - Visit a museum or a zoo.
  - Go to a yard sale or auction.
  - Go rollerskating or rollerblading with a friend.
  - Drop by a health food store and walk the aisles.

CARPE DIEM:
Plan a mini-vacation for today. Spend one
hour doing something special.

39.

SAY NO.

- Especially soon after the death, you may lack the energy as well as the desire to participate in activities you used to find pleasurable.

- It's OK to say no when you're asked to help with a project or attend a party.

- Write a note to the people who've invited you and explain your feelings. Be sure to thank them for the invitation.

- Realize that you can't keep saying no forever. There will always be that first wedding, christening, birthday party, etc. Don't miss out on life's most joyful celebrations.

CARPE DIEM:
Say no to something today. Allow yourself
not to feel guilty about it.

40.

BE MINDFUL OF ANNIVERSARIES.

- Anniversaries—of the death, life events, birthdays—can be especially hard when you are in grief.

- These are times you may want to plan ahead for.

- Perhaps you could take a day off work on the anniversary of the death. Maybe you could visit the cemetery on the next birthday of the person who died.

- Reach out to others on these difficult days. Talk about your feelings with a close friend.

CARPE DIEM:

What's the next anniversary you've been anticipating? Make a plan right now for what you will do on that day. Enlist a friend's help so you won't be alone.

41.

SET ASIDE THE ANNIVERSARY OF THE DEATH AS A HOLIDAY.

- Perhaps you dread the anniversary of the death. Many of us feel particularly sad and alone on this day.

- Consider setting aside the anniversary as an annual holiday. Each year, visit the grave. Perhaps plan a ceremony with friends and family.

- Commemorate the life that was lived by doing something the person who died would have appreciated.

- You might want to spend this day in the company of others who love you.

CARPE DIEM:
Call three other people who loved the person who died and plan an activity or ceremony for the anniversary of the death.

42.

PREPARE YOURSELF FOR THE HOLIDAYS.

- Because the person who died is no longer there to share the holidays with, you may feel particularly sad and vulnerable during Thanksgiving, Christmas or Hanukkah and other holidays.

- Don't overextend yourself during the holidays.

- Don't feel you have to shop, bake, entertain, send cards, etc. if you're not up for it.

- Sometimes old holiday rituals are comforting after a death and sometimes they're not. Continue them only if they feel good to you; consider creating new ones, as well.

CARPE DIEM:

What's the next major holiday? Make a game plan right now and let those you usually spend the day with know of your plan well in advance.

43.

GO SHOPPING.

- Shopping involves getting dressed and going out into the world. Sometimes pushing yourself to do just this much will help you have a better day.

- Shop somewhere you usually don't. Browse through an antique shop or flea market. Visit an art gallery. Drive to the mall two towns over.

- Pile up your mail order catalogs next to a comfy chair and spend all day lingering over each and every one.

- If you tend to buy things to fill some emotional need, don't go shopping. Instead, make a list of everything you've purchased in the last six months. Then consider how you feel about those purchases today.

CARPE DIEM:
Buy yourself something that makes you
feel good, even if it's frivolous.

44.

KNOW THAT GRIEF DOES NOT PROCEED IN ORDERLY, PREDICTABLE "STAGES."

- Though the "Needs of Mourning" (Ideas 3-8) are numbered 1-6, grief is not an orderly progression towards healing. Don't fall into the trap of thinking your grief journey will be predictable or always forward-moving.

- Usually, grief hurts more before it hurts less.

- You will probably experience a multitude of different emotions in a wave-like fashion. You will also likely encounter more than one need of mourning at the same time.

- Be compassionate with yourself as you experience your own unique grief journey.

CARPE DIEM:
Has anyone told you that you are in this or that "stage" of grief? Ignore this usually well-intentioned advice. Don't allow yourself or anyone else to compartmentalize your grief.

45.

TALK OUT LOUD TO
THE PERSON WHO DIED.

- Sometimes it feels good to talk to the person who died.

- Pretend he's sitting in the chair across from you and tell him how you're doing.

- Talk to photos of the person who died. Share your deepest thoughts and feelings with him. Make it part of your daily routine to say "Good morning!" to that photo on your nightstand.

- Visit the cemetery (or columbarium or scattering place if the person was cremated) and if you're not too self-conscious, talk to the person you loved so much.

CARPE DIEM:
If you haven't already, put a photo of the person who died in your wallet or purse. Make it a habit to look at the photo and tell the person what's going on in your life that day.

46.

MAKE A LIST OF GOALS.

- While you should not set a particular time and course for your healing, it may help you to make other life goals for the coming year.

- Make a list of short-term goals for the next three months. Perhaps some of the goals could have to do with mourning activities (e.g. make a memory book).

- Also make a list of long-term goals for the next year.

- Be both realistic and compassionate with yourself as you consider what's feasible and feels good and what will only add too much stress to your life.

CARPE DIEM:

Write a list of goals for this week. Your goals may be as simple as: Go to work every day. Tell John I love him once a day. Take a walk on Tuesday night.

47.

MAKE SOMETHING FROM SCRATCH.

- Making something to eat from scratch can be a lot of work, but it can also be a very satisfying and fun activity.

- Baking bread is good therapy. If you've never done it before, don't worry—just follow a recipe!

- Other "from scratch" ideas: bake a cake; make soup stock; make homemade pasta noodles; make your own pizza.

CARPE DIEM:
Make a double batch of your favorite cookie.
Keep half and give half to a neighbor or friend.

48.

PLANT SEEDS OF HOPE.

- Gardening represents growth, beauty and the natural cycles of life and death.

- Indoors or out, gardening is often healing for mourners.

- If you already garden, allocate some extra time for digging in the dirt this season. Perhaps plan a new perennial bed or plant some bulbs.

- Non-gardeners might start with a container garden or an indoor plant.

CARPE DIEM:
Visit a local nursery or arboretum and spend some
time learning about what you see there.

49.

GO TO A FARMER'S MARKET.

- We tend not to eat well when we're in mourning. This lack of good nutrition contributes to our feelings of listlessness and fatigue.

- Vegetables and fruits have amazing restorative powers.

- Go to your local farmer's market and buy whatever's in season. Prepare it simply and quickly, while it's still fresh.

- Off season, visit the produce department of your area's best grocery store. Select an assortment of fresh fruits and vegetables.

CARPE DIEM:

Eat five servings of fresh vegetables and three of fresh fruit today. Make a huge salad or a fruit smoothie in your blender.

50.

SUBSCRIBE TO HEALING.

- There are a number of healing magazines for mourners. Most include mourner's stories of loss and renewed hope, poetry, meaningful artwork.

- One of this author's favorites is *Bereavement*, a bimonthly magazine filled with personal stories of loss and healing, grief education, poetry, etc. At the time of this writing, a one-year subscription within the U.S. costs $32 and can be ordered through the Center for Loss and Life Transition, (970) 226-6050.

- Instead of a grief magazine, consider a magazine you've always wanted to read but have never allowed yourself the time to.

CARPE DIEM:
Call the number above and start a subscription today.

51.

IDENTITY THREE PEOPLE YOU CAN TURN TO ANYTIME YOU NEED A FRIEND.

- You may have many people who care about you but few who are able to be good companions in grief.

- Identify three people whom you think can be there for you in the coming weeks and months.

- Don't assume that others will help.

- Even normally compassionate people sometimes find it hard to be present to others in grief.

CARPE DIEM:
Call these three people and ask them outright: Are you willing to help me with my grief? Tell them you mainly need to spend time with them and to talk to them freely.

52.

TAKE A RISK.

- For some, activities that harbor risk, real or perceived, are invigorating and life-affirming.

- Sometimes people who've encountered death, in particular, feel ready to try limit-stretching activities.

- Some ideas: hang gliding, bungee jumping, skydiving, rock climbing.

- Don't confuse appropriate risk-taking with self-destructiveness. Never test your own mortality through inappropriate behaviors or inadequate safeguards.

CARPE DIEM:
Schedule a sunrise hot air balloon ride with a trained, licensed balloonist. Toast the dawn with champagne at 5,000 feet.

53.

PICTURE THIS.

- The visual arts have a way of making us see the world anew.

- Perhaps you would enjoy a visit to an art gallery or museum, a sculpture garden, a photography exhibit.

- Why not try to create some art yourself? Attend a watercolor or calligraphy class.

- Making pottery is something almost everyone has fun trying. It's tactile and messy and whimsical.

CARPE DIEM:
Buy some paints, some brushes and a canvas and paint your feelings about the death. Don't worry about your artistic abilities; just let your imagination take charge.

54.

LAUGH.

- Humor is one of the most healing gifts of humanity.

- Laughter restores hope and assists us in surviving the pain of grief.

- Rent a cornball comedy and invite a friend over for popcorn and a few giggles.

- Get tickets to a stand-up comedy routine. Watch a slapstick TV show, like The Three Stooges or America's Funniest Home Videos.

CARPE DIEM:

Watch cartoons this morning. Looney Tunes are usually good for a laugh, and with Cartoon Network and videos at your local movie store, you should be able to watch them anytime, anywhere.

55.

PRACTICE PATIENCE.

- The quality of patience will serve you well as you experience your grief and mourning.

- We need to slow down, to turn inward and experience our feelings of loss.

- Our society is constantly trying to speed up our grief.

- Practicing patience opens your heart to the present moment and allows healing and joy into your life.

CARPE DIEM:

Write the following saying somewhere that you will see it each day: "There are no rewards given for how fast I grieve and mourn. I must be compassionate with myself." Repeat these words out loud to yourself every day for the next 2 weeks.

56.

MOVE TOWARD YOUR GRIEF, NOT AWAY FROM IT.

- Our society teaches us that emotional pain is to be avoided, not embraced, yet it is only in moving toward our grief that we can be healed.

- As Helen Keller once said, "The only way to get to the other side is to go through the door."

- Be alert to people who tell you to"keep real busy." Keeping real busy will keep you from your grief and mourning.

- As you move toward your feelings of loss, you'll need to do so in "doses." You cannot (nor should you try to) do it all at once.

CARPE DIEM:

Today, talk to someone else who loved the person who died. Share your thoughts and feelings with her openly and encourage her to do the same. Support each other in your grief.

57.

DON'T EXPECT YOURSELF TO MOURN OR HEAL IN A CERTAIN WAY OR IN A CERTAIN TIME.

- Your unique grief journey will be shaped by many factors, including:
  - the nature of the relationship you had with the person who died.
  - the age of the person who died.
  - the circumstances of the death.
  - your unique personality.
  - your cultural background.
  - your religious or spiritual beliefs.
  - your gender.
  - your support systems.

- Because of these and other factors, no two deaths are ever mourned in precisely the same way.

- Don't have rigid expectations for your thoughts, feelings and behaviors.

CARPE DIEM:
Draw two columns on a piece of paper. Title the left column "What I used to think grief would be like." Title the right column "What it's really like." Jot down notes in both columns.

58.

TELL THE STORY, OVER AND OVER AGAIN IF NECESSARY.

- Acknowledging a death is a painful, ongoing task that we accomplish in doses, over time. A vital part of healing in grief is often "telling the story" over and over again.

- The "story" relates the circumstances surrounding the death, reviewing the relationship, describing aspects of the personality of the person who died, and sharing memories, good and bad.

- It's as if each time we tell the story, it becomes a little more real.

- Find people who are willing to listen to you tell your story, over and over again if necessary, without judgment..

CARPE DIEM:
Tell the story to someone today in the form of
a letter. Perhaps you can write and send this letter
to a friend who lives far away.

59.

GET AWAY FROM IT ALL.

- Sometimes it takes a change of scenery to reveal the texture of our lives.

- New people and places help us see our lives from a new vantage point and can assist us in our search for meaning.

- Often, getting away from it all means leaving civilization behind and retreating to nature. But it can also mean temporarily abandoning your environment and spending time in one that's altogether different.

- Visit a foreign country. Go backpacking in the wilderness. Spend a weekend at a bed and breakfast.

CARPE DIEM:
Plan a trip to somewhere far away.
Ask a friend to travel with you.

60.

ESTABLISH A MEMORIAL FUND IN THE NAME OF THE PERSON WHO DIED.

- Sometimes bereaved families ask that memorial contributions be made to specified charities in the name of the person who died. This practice allows friends and family members to show their support while helping the family feel that something good came of the death.

- You can establish a personalized and ongoing memorial to the person who died.

- What was meaningful to the person who died? Did she support a certain nonprofit organization or participate in a certain recreational activity? Was she politically active or affected by a certain illness?

- Your local bank or funeral home may have ideas about how to go about setting up a memorial fund.

CARPE DIEM:

Call another friend of the person who died and together brainstorm a list of ideas for a memorial. Suggest that both of you commit to making at least one additional phone call for information before the day is out.

61.

BRIGHTEN UP YOUR ENVIRONMENT.

- Would your home or office benefit from a little sprucing up?

- Paint your living room or office in a fresh, new color. Paint is inexpensive and easy to redo.

- Sometimes something as minor as new valances and freshly cleaned windowpanes can make a big difference.

- Place some fresh flowers somewhere you will see them throughout the day.

CARPE DIEM:
Buy yourself a new set of sumptuous, all-cotton bed sheets in your favorite color or an appropriate pattern. Don't worry if they don't match your bedroom; no interior decorating rules apply today!

62.

SURF THE WEB.

- The World Wide Web has a number of interesting and informative resources for mourners.

- Many articles about grief are available online. Books can also be purchased online. Most grief organizations (MADD, Compassionate Friends, Widowed Persons Service) now have Web pages.

- Search the word "grief" and see what you find. Use a more specific term (widow, AIDS, etc.) if appropriate.

- Like face-to-face support groups, Internet chat groups can be healing for mourners.

CARPE DIEM:
Sit down at your computer today and do a search.
If you don't own a computer or have access to one at work,
visit your local library. Don't forget to visit the
Center for Loss Web site: www.centerforloss.com.

63.

FOLLOW YOUR NOSE.

- For centuries people have understood that certain smells induce certain feelings. Aromatherapy is the contemporary term for this age-old practice.

- Some comforting, memory-inducing smells include baby powder, freshly cut grass, dill, oranges, leather, lilacs.

- Essential oils, available at your local drugstore or bath and body shop, can be added to bath water or dabbed lightly on pulse points.

- Lavender relaxes. Rosewood and bergamot together lift the spirits. Peppermint invigorates. Chamomile and lavender are sleep aids.

CARPE DIEM:
Visit a local bath and body shop and choose one or two essential oils or scented candles. Try using them today.

64.

LISTEN TO THE MUSIC.

- During times of grief, music can be very healing because it helps us access our feelings, both happy and sad. Music can soothe the spirit and nurture the heart.

- All types of music can be healing—rock & roll, classical, blues, folk.

- Consider listening to music you normally don't, perhaps the opera or the symphony. Or make a recording of your favorite songs, all together on one tape.

- Do you play an instrument or sing? Allow yourself the time to try these activities again soon.

CARPE DIEM:
Visit a music store today and sample a few CDs or cassettes.
Buy yourself the one that moves you the most.

65.

THINK YOUNG.

- It is the nature of children to live for the moment and appreciate today. All of us would benefit from a little more childlike wonder.

- Do something childish—blow bubbles, skip rope, visit a toy store, build a sand castle, fly a kite, climb a tree.

- If kids aren't already a part of your life, make arrangements to spend some time with them.

- Volunteer at a local school. Take a friend's children to the park one afternoon.

CARPE DIEM:
Buy a gift for a child today just because.

66.

PRAY.

- Studies have shown that prayer can help people heal.

- If you believe in a higher power, pray.

- Pray for the person who died. Pray for your questions about life and death to be answered. Pray for the strength to embrace your pain and to heal over time. Pray for others affected by this death.

- Many churches have prayer lists. Call your church and ask that your name be added to the prayer list. On Sundays, the whole congregation will pray for you. Often many individuals will pray at home for those on the prayer list, as well.

CARPE DIEM:
Bow your head right now and say a silent prayer.
If you are out of practice, don't worry; just let
your thoughts flow naturally.

67.

TAKE A BUBBLE BATH.

- In our hurry-up world, showers are usually the order of the day. We often don't allow time for the pleasure of taking a long, hot, bubbly bath.

- Draw a hot, hot bath. Pour in some bath salts, oils or bubbles.

- Place lit candles around the bathroom (safely!). Turn off the overhead lights.

- Soak until the water grows tepid. Clear your mind and focus on the sensation of the water lapping around you.

CARPE DIEM:
Buy bubble bath "paints," which are available in many children's departments. Have fun in the tub painting yourself or the walls around your tub

68.

VISIT THE CEMETERY.

- Visiting the cemetery is an important mourning ritual. It helps us embrace our loss and remember the person who died.

- Memorial Day, Veteran's Day, Labor Day, Mother's Day or Father's Day are traditional days to visit the cemetery and pay respects.

- If the body was cremated, you may want to visit the scattering site or columbarium.

- Ask a friend or family member to go with you. You may feel comforted by their presence. Or, if it feels right for you, go alone and sit in sacred silence.

CARPE DIEM:

If you can, drop by the cemetery today with a nosegay of fresh flowers. Scatter the petals over the grave.

69.

PUBLISH A VERSE IN YOUR LOCAL NEWSPAPER.

- Sometimes friends or family of the person who died will publish a memorial poem in the newspaper as a way of honoring the death and bearing witness to their grief.

- Write your own poem or find one in a book at the library.

- Verses often appear on the anniversary of the death or the birthday of the person who died.

- Such verses are often published in or near the obituaries or the classified section of the newspaper.

CARPE DIEM:
Call your local newspaper and ask for rates and suggestions on publishing a memorial verse.

70.

ORGANIZE A TREE PLANTING.

- Trees represent the beauty, vibrancy and continuity of life.

- A specially planted and located tree can honor the person who died and serve as a perennial memorial.

- You might write a short ceremony for the tree planting. (Or ask a friend to write one.) Consider a personalized metal marker or sign, too.

- For a more private option, plant a tree in your own yard. Consult your local nursery for an appropriate selection. Flowering trees are especially beautiful in the spring.

CARPE DIEM:

Order a tree for your own yard and plant it in honor of the person who died. You'll probably need someone to help you prepare the hole and place the tree.

71.

GET UP WITH THE BIRDS.

- The sun is a powerful symbol of life and renewal.

- When was the last time you watched the sun rise? Do you remember being touched by its beauty and power?

- Plan an early morning breakfast or walk in a location where you can see the sun rise. Hike to the top of a hill. Have coffee on a patio next to a lake.

- Sometimes you may have trouble sleeping and may be up early anyway. Invite a friend to share the dawn with you.

CARPE DIEM:
Invite a friend on an early morning drive. Choose a fitting destination for watching the sun rise. Pack a brunch of hot coffee, rolls, fresh fruit.

72.

REASSESS YOUR PRIORITIES.

- Death has a way of making us rethink our priorities and redefines the meaning of our lives.

- What gives your life meaning? What doesn't?

- Take steps to spend more of your time on the former and less on the latter.

- Now may be the time to reconfigure your life. Choose a satisfying new career. Go back to school. Begin volunteering. Move closer to your family.

CARPE DIEM:
Make a list with two columns: What's important to me. What's not. Brainstorm for at least 15 minutes.

73.

TAKE SOME TIME OFF WORK.

- Typically, our society grants us three days "bereavement leave" and then expects us to return to work as if nothing happened.

- As you know, three days is a paltry allowance for grief. Talk to your supervisor about taking off some additional time following the death.

- Some companies will grant extended leaves of absence or sabbaticals in some situations.

- If you simply can't take off additional time, request that your work load be lightened for the next several months.

CARPE DIEM:
Take a mental health day today and call in sick.
Spend the day resting or doing something you enjoy.

74.

DON'T BE CAUGHT OFF GUARD BY "GRIEFBURSTS."

- Sometimes heightened periods of sadness overwhelm us when we're in grief.

- These times can seem to come of out nowhere and can be frightening and painful.

- Even long after the death, something as simple as a sound, a smell or a phrase can bring on a "griefburst."

- Allow yourself to experience griefbursts without shame or self-judgment, no matter where and when they occur. If you would feel more comfortable, retreat to somewhere private when these strong feelings surface.

CARPE DIEM:
Create an action plan for your next griefburst. For example, you might plan to drop whatever you are doing and go for a walk or record thoughts in your journal.

75.

GET A NEW HAIRCUT,
HIGHLIGHT OR COLOR.

- Sometimes when we're in mourning we feel dull and unattractive. Our self-esteem can be affected by our grief.

- You may not be bothering with your appearance because of your low energy.

- Part of good self-care and healing is learning to love and value our lives again, including our physical selves.

- Take a look in the mirror and compassionately reacquaint yourself with you.

CARPE DIEM:
Today, schedule an appointment for a new haircut, highlight or color. Get a facial and manicure, too, if your budget permits.

76.

TURN TO YOUR FAMILY.

- In today's mobile, disconnected society, many people have lost touch with the gift of family. Your friends may come and go, but family, as they say, is forever.

- If you're emotionally close to members of your family, you're probably already reaching out to them for support. Allow them to be there for you. Let them in.

- If you're not emotionally close to your family, perhaps now is the time to open closed doors. Call a family member you haven't spoken to for a while. Hop in a car or on a plane and make a long overdue visit.

- Don't feel bad if you have to be the initiator; instead, expend your energy by writing that first letter or making that first phone call.

CARPE DIEM:
Call a family member you feel close to today.
Make plans to visit this person soon.

77.

SPEND TIME ALONE.

- Reaching out to others while we're in mourning is necessary. Mourning is hard work and you can't get through it by yourself.

- Still, you will also need alone time as you work on the six needs of mourning. To slow down and to turn inward, you must sometimes insist on solitude.

- Schedule alone time into each week. Go for a walk in the woods. Lock your bedroom door and read a book. Work in your garden.

- Don't shut your friends and family out altogether, but do heed the call for contemplative silence.

CARPE DIEM:
Schedule one hour of solitude into your day today.

78.

LEARN TO MEDITATE.

- Meditation is simply quiet, relaxed contemplation.

- You needn't follow any particular rules or techniques. Simply find a quiet place where you can think without distraction and rid your mind of superficial thoughts and concerns.

- Relax your muscles and close your eyes if you'd like.

- Try meditating for 10-15 minutes each day. It may help center you and provide a good outlet for your grief.

CARPE DIEM:
Try reflecting on this thought: "As I allow myself to mourn, I create an opening in my heart. Releasing the tensions of grief, surrendering to the struggle, means freeing myself to go forward."

79.

PAY SOMEONE TO CLEAN YOUR HOUSE.

- When in grief, we can easily be overwhelmed by the many tasks of daily living.

- Cleaning can feel particularly burdensome right now.

- Here's a thought: Don't clean this week! The health inspector probably won't shut you down, at least not for another month or two.

- One of your friends might be looking for a way to help. Ask him to help with occasional cleaning.

CARPE DIEM:
Call a maid service and schedule someone to come to your house for a half day this week. Provide her with a list of the top 10 things you'd like to have taken care of.

80.

DESIGNATE A TIME TO
MOURN EACH DAY.

- Consider making mourning part of your daily routine, just like taking a shower or reading the newspaper.

- Set aside a quiet time each day for embracing your thoughts and feelings about the death.

- The first 10 minutes after you wake up might work.
  This also might be a good time to journal your thoughts and feelings.

- Sometimes creating a dedicated mourning time allows you to concentrate on living the rest of your day.

CARPE DIEM:
Schedule a "mourning time" for tomorrow.
Write it down in your daily planner.

81.

SCHEDULE SOMETHING THAT GIVES YOU PLEASURE EACH AND EVERY DAY.

- Often mourners need something to look forward to, a reason to get out of bed today.

- It's hard to look forward to each day when you know you will be experiencing pain and sadness.

- To counterbalance your normal and necessary mourning, plan something you enjoy doing every day.

- Read, bake, go for a walk, have lunch with a friend, play computer games—do whatever brings you enjoyment.

CARPE DIEM:
What's on tap for today? Squeeze in something you enjoy, no matter how hectic your schedule.

82.

JOIN THE CLUB.

- You may benefit from regular participation in social organizations because they provide friendship, routine, plans for the future.

- Book discussion groups, Kiwanis, singing groups, environmental organizations are just a few ideas.

- Political groups and human service organizations (Sierra Club, United Way, etc.) can provide a sense of purpose and satisfaction.

CARPE DIEM:
Check your local paper for a listing of
club and organization meetings. Circle two or
three and call the contact person for more information.

83.

GO TO THE MOVIES.

- Movies aren't just for entertainment. They're often a window into the experiences, thoughts and feelings of others.

- The stories we see on the big screen can give us insight into our own lives.

- Sometimes movies about loss and healing are helpful to mourners, e.g. *Shadowlands* or *The Joy Luck Club*.

- Consider drive-in movies, art films, IMAX and other out-of-the-ordinary film venues.

CARPE DIEM:
Rent a comedic film tonight, pop popcorn and share the evening with a good friend. As a therapist I can highly recommend *What About Bob?* for a good laugh.

84.

RECONNECT WITH SOMEONE SPECIAL.

- Throughout our lives, we often lose contact with people who've touched us or made a difference somehow.

- Death can make us realize that keeping in touch with these people is well worth the effort.

- Whom have you loved or admired but haven't spoken with for a long time?

- To wit: teachers, old lovers, childhood friends, past neighbors.

CARPE DIEM:
Write a letter to someone you haven't been in touch with for a long time. Track down her address and phone number. Catch her up on your life and invite her to do the same by calling you or writing you back.

85.

LET GO OF DESTRUCTIVE MYTHS ABOUT GRIEF AND MOURNING.

- You have probably internalized many of our society's harmful myths about grief and mourning.

- Here are some to let go of:
  - I need to be strong and carry on.
  - Tears are a sign of weakness.
  - I need to get over my grief.
  - Death is something we don't talk about.

- Sometimes these myths will cause you to feel guilty about or ashamed of your true thoughts and feelings.

- Your grief is your grief. It's normal and necessary. Allow it to be what it is.

CARPE DIEM:
Write out a list of any harmful myths you may have been taught. Find a friend to discuss how these myths may be influencing your grief journey.

86.

WATCH FOR WARNING SIGNS.

- Sometimes mourners fall back on self-destructive behaviors to get through this difficult time.

- Try to be honest with yourself about drug or alcohol abuse. If you're in over your head, ask someone for help.

- Are you having suicidal thoughts and feelings? Are you isolating yourself too much? Talk to someone today.

- Getting help is a form of compassionate self-care.

CARPE DIEM:

Acknowledging to ourselves that we have a problem may come too late. If someone suggests that you need help, consider yourself lucky to be so well-loved and get help.

87.

LEARN SOMETHING NEW.

- Perhaps you would enjoy learning something new or trying a new hobby.

- What have you always wanted to learn but have never tried? Playing the guitar? Woodworking? Speaking French?

- Consider physical activities. Learning to play golf or doing karate have the added benefits of exercise.

- Turn to trusted friends to suggest creative ideas for new activities.

CARPE DIEM:
Check your local community calendar and sign up for a class in something you have never tried before.

88.

VOLUNTEER.

- Consider honoring the death through social activism. If the person who died was a victim of drunk driving, participate in a local MADD rally. If your baby was stillborn, collect in your neighborhood for The March of Dimes' annual campaign.

- Volunteer at a senior center, an elementary school, a local hospital—someplace befitting the person who died.

- If your schedule is too hectic and you can afford it, offer money instead of time.

- Make your donation in memory of the person who died.

CARPE DIEM:
Call your local United Way and ask for some suggestions about upcoming events you could participate in.

89.

PLAN A CEREMONY.

- When words are inadequate, have ceremony.

- Ceremony assists in reality, recall, support, expression, transcendence.

- When personalized, the funeral ceremony can be a healing ritual. But ceremonies that take place later on can also be very meaningful.

- The ceremony might center on memories of the person who died, "meaning of life" thoughts and feelings or affirmation of faith.

CARPE DIEM:
Offer to hold a candle-lighting memory ceremony.
With a small group of friends, form a circle. Each person
holds and lights their own candle while sharing a memory
of the person who died. At the end, read a poem or
prayer in memory of the person who died.

90.

ORGANIZE A MEMORY BOOK.

- Assembling a scrapbook that holds treasured photos and mementos of the person who died can be a very healing activity.

- You might consider including a birth certificate, school work, newspaper clippings, locks of hair, old letters.

- Phone others who loved the person who died and ask them to write a note or contribute photos.

- Other ideas: a memory box, photo buttons of the person who died (nice for a child or younger person), a memory quilt.

CARPE DIEM:
Buy an appropriate scrapbook or keepsake box today. Don't forget to buy the associated materials you'll need, such as photo pages or photo corners, glue, scissors, etc.

91.

VISIT THE GREAT OUTDOORS.

- For many people it is restorative and energizing to spend time outside.

- When we are in grief, we often find nature's timeless beauty healing. The sound of a bird singing or the awesome presence of an old tree can help put things in perspective.

- Go on a nature walk. Or camping. Or canoeing. The farther away from civilization the better.

CARPE DIEM:

Call your area forest service for a map of nearby walking or hiking trails. Take a hike sometime this week.

92.

MAKE A LIST OF YOUR LOSSES.

- When you're feeling overwhelmed by your feelings of grief and loss, sometimes it helps to articulate those feelings to yourself.

- Make a list of the losses you're experiencing:
  When Mary died, I lost:
    - my wife
    - my best friend
    - the mother of my children
    - the person who kept this house running
    - my dancing partner
    - my safety, security
    - some of the meaning and purpose in my life

- Don't stop until you've explored the many aspects of your loss.

CARPE DIEM:
Right now, brainstorm a list of your losses. Talk to someone about your list after you've finished.

93.

ALLOW FOR FEELINGS OF UNFINISHED BUSINESS.

* Death often brings about feelings of unfinished business. Things we never did, things we didn't get to say, things we wish we hadn't.

* Allow yourself to think and feel through these "if onlys." You may never be able to fully resolve these issues, but if you permit yourself to mourn them, you will be become reconciled to them.

* Is there something you wanted to say to the person who died but never did? Write him a letter that openly expresses your thoughts and feelings.

CARPE DIEM:
Perhaps the person who died left some task incomplete. Finish it on his behalf.

94.

HELP OTHERS.

- Help others! But I'm the one who needs help right now, you may be thinking.

- It's true, you do deserve special compassion and attention right now. But often, people find healing in selflessness.

- Consider volunteering at a nursing home, a homeless shelter, your neighborhood school.

- If you're well into your grief journey, you may find yourself ready and able to help other mourners by starting a support group or volunteering at a hospice.

CARPE DIEM:
Do something nice for someone who would never expect it.

95.

TEACH OTHERS ABOUT GRIEF AND MOURNING.

- To love is to one day mourn. You have learned this most poignant of life's lessons.

- Maybe you could teach what you are learning to others. Tell your friends and family about the six needs of mourning. Teach them how they can best support you.

- Share your wisdom in the safety of a grief support group.

- Remember that each person's grief is unique. Your experiences will not be shared or appreciated by everyone.

CARPE DIEM:
Buy a friend the companion book to this one, called *"Healing A Friend's Grieving Heart: 100 Practical Ideas for Helping Someone You Love Through Loss."* It provides concise grief education and practical tips for helping.

96.

COUNT YOUR BLESSINGS.

- You may not be feeling very good about your life right now. That's OK.

- Still, you are blessed. Your life has purpose and meaning. It will just take you some time to think and feel this through for yourself.

- This is not to deny the hurt, for the hurt needs to take precedence right now. But it may help to consider the things that make your life worth living, too.

- Attempt to spend time around people who allow you to feel your sadness, yet give you a sense of hope for your healing.

CARPE DIEM:

If you're feeling ready, make a list of the blessings in your life: your family, your friends, your job, your house. Be specific. "I'm thankful for John's smile. My Wenlock roses. The way the sun slants through my kitchen window in the morning."

97.

KNOW THAT YOU ARE LOVED.

- Love gives our lives meaning. Look around you for expressions of care and concern.

- There are people who love you. There are people who want to be an important part of your support system.

- Some of those who love you may not know how to reach out to you in grief, but they still love you.

- Think about the people who care about you and the ways in which your life matters.

CARPE DIEM:

Get out some of the notes and cards you have received from people who care about you. Re-read them and remind yourself that you are loved.

98.

PRACTICE BREATHING
IN AND OUT.

- Sometimes what we need most is just to "be." In our goal-oriented society, many of us have lost the knack for simply living.

- Drop all your plans and obligations for today and do nothing.

- Meditate if meditation helps center you.

- Find someplace quiet, be still, close your eyes and focus on breathing in and out. Relax your muscles. Listen to your own heartbeat.

CARPE DIEM:
Sit down, focus on something 20-30 feet
away and take 10 deep breaths.

99.

UNDERSTAND THE CONCEPT OF "RECONCILIATION."

- Sometimes you'll hear about mourners "recovering" from grief. This term is damaging because it implies that grief is an illness that must be cured. It also connotes a return to the way things were before the death.

- Mourners don't recover from grief. We become "reconciled" to it. In other words, we learn to live with it and are forever changed by it.

- This does not mean a life of misery, however. We often not only heal but grow through grief. Our lives can potentially be deeper and more meaningful after the death of someone loved.

- Reconciliation takes time. You may not become truly reconciled to your loss for several years and even then will have "griefbursts" forever.

CARPE DIEM:

Write down the following words somewhere you will see them often: "Mourning never really completely ends, only as time goes on and I do my mourning work, it erupts less frequently."

100.

STRIVE TO GROW
THROUGH GRIEF.

- You may find that you are growing emotionally and spiritually as a result of your grief journey.

- Growth means a new inner balance with no end points. While you may do the work of mourning to recapture in part some sense of inner balance, it is a new inner balance.

- Growth means exploring our assumptions about life. Ultimately, exploring our assumptions about life after the death of someone loved can make those assumptions richer and more life-affirming.

- Growth means utilizing our potentials. The encounter of grief reawakens us to the importance of utilizing our potentials—our capacities to mourn our losses openly and without shame, to be interpersonally effective in our relationships with others, and to continue to discover fulfillment in life, living and loving.

CARPE DIEM:
Consider the ways in which you may
be "growing through grief."

A FINAL WORD

It is in suffering that we are withdrawn from the bright superficial film of existence, from the sway of time and mere things, and find ourselves in the presence of a profounder truth.

Yves M. Congar
God, Man and the Universe

We have all heard the words "Blessed are those who mourn, for they shall be comforted." To this I might add, "Blessed are those who learn self-compassion during times of grief, for they shall go on to discover continued meaning in life, living and loving."

I can't say enough about the importance of self-care during this time. Remember—it is not selfish or self-indulgent. Instead, self-care fortifies you for the ongoing ebbs and flows of your grief journey, a journey which leaves you profoundly affected and deeply changed. To be self-nurturing is to have the courage to pay attention to your needs. Above all, self-nurturing is about self-acceptance. When we recognize that self-care begins with ourselves, we no longer think of those around as being totally responsible for our well-being. Healthy self-care frees us to mourn in ways that help us heal, and that is nurturing indeed.

I also believe self-nurturing is about celebration, taking time to enjoy the moment, to find hidden treasures everywhere—a child's smile, a beautiful sunrise, a flower in bloom, a friend's gentle touch. Grief teaches us the importance of living fully in the present, remembering our past, and embracing our future.

Walt Whitman wrote "I celebrate myself." In caring for yourself "with passion" you are celebrating life as a human being who has been touched by grief and come to recognize that the preciousness of life is a superb opportunity for celebration!

Grief teaches us that there is so much to know about ourselves and the world around us. But to be open to that knowledge demands that we slow down, turn inward, and seek self-support as well as outside support.

Grief teaches us that we need to simplify our lives to be open to giving and receiving love. We need a sense of belonging, a sense of meaning, a sense of purpose. Realizing that we belong helps us feel safe and secure.

Grief teaches us we have only now to let people know that we love them. There is magic and miracles in loving and being loved. One final "carpe diem" for you: Call someone right now and let them know how their kindness and love sustain you.

Bless you. I hope we meet one day.

THE MOURNER'S CODE

Ten Self-Compassionate Principles

Though you should reach out to others as you journey through grief, you should not feel obligated to accept the unhelpful responses you may receive from some people. You are the one who is grieving, and as such, you have certain "rights" no one should try to take away from you.

The following list is intended both to empower you to heal and to decide how others can and cannot help. This is not to discourage you from reaching out to others for help, but rather to assist you in distinguishing useful responses from hurtful ones.

1. **You have the right to experience your own unique grief.**
   No one else will grieve in exactly the same way you do. So, when you turn to others for help, don't allow them to tell you what you should or should not be feeling.

2. **You have the right to talk about your grief.**
   Talking about your grief will help you heal. Seek out others who will allow you to talk as much as you want, as often as you want, about your grief. If at times you don't feel like talking, you also have the right to be silent.

3. **You have the right to feel a multitude of emotions.**
   Confusion, disorientation, fear, guilt and relief are just a few of the emotions you might feel as part of your grief journey. Others may try to tell you that feeling angry, for

example, is wrong. Don't take these judgmental responses to heart. Instead, find listeners who will accept your feelings without condition.

4. You have the right to be tolerant of your physical and emotional limits.
Your feelings of loss and sadness will probably leave you feeling fatigued. Respect what your body and mind are telling you. Get daily rest. Eat balanced meals. And don't allow others to push you into doing things you don't feel ready to do.

5. You have the right to experience "griefbursts."
Sometimes, out of nowhere, a powerful surge of grief may overcome you. This can be frightening, but is normal and natural. Find someone who understands and will let you talk it out.

6. You have the right to make use of ritual.
The funeral ritual does more than acknowledge the death of someone loved. It helps provide you with the support of caring people. More importantly, the funeral is a way for you to mourn. If others tell you the funeral or other healing rituals such as these are silly or unnecessary, don't listen.

7. You have the right to embrace your spirituality.
If faith is a part of your life, express it in ways that seem appropriate to you. Allow yourself to be around people who understand and support your religious beliefs. If you feel angry at God, find someone to talk with who won't be critical of your feelings of hurt and abandonment.

8. You have the right to search for meaning.

You may find yourself asking, "Why did he or she die? Why this way? Why now?" Some of your questions may have answers, but some may not. And watch out for the clichéd responses some people may give you. Comments like, "It was God's will" or "Think of what you still have to be thankful for" are not helpful and you do not have to accept them.

9. You have the right to treasure your memories.

Memories are one of the best legacies that exist after the death of someone loved. You will always remember. Instead of ignoring your memories, find others with whom you can share them.

10. You have the right to move toward your grief and heal.

Reconciling your grief will not happen quickly. Remember, grief is a process, not an event. Be patient and tolerant with yourself and avoid people who are impatient and intolerant with you. Neither you nor those around you must forget that the death of someone loved changes your life forever.

SEND US YOUR IDEAS FOR
HEALING YOUR GRIEVING HEART!

I'd love to hear your practical ideas for being self-compassionate in grief. I may use them in future editions of this book or in other publications through the Center for Loss. Please jot down your idea and mail it to:

Dr. Alan Wolfelt
The Center for Loss and Life Transition
3735 Broken Bow Rd.
Fort Collins, CO 80526
wolfelt@centerforloss.com

I look forward to hearing from you!

My idea:

_____

_____

_____

_____

_____

_____

_____

My name and mailing address:

_____

_____

_____

_____

ALSO BY ALAN WOLFELT

HEALING A FRIEND'S GRIEVING HEART: 100 PRACTICAL IDEAS FOR HELPING SOMEONE YOU LOVE THROUGH LOSS

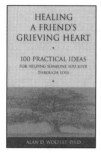

When a friend suffers the loss of someone loved, you may not always know what to say: But you can do many helpful, loving things. Compassionate and eminently practical, *Healing A Friend's Grieving Heart* offers 100 fresh ideas for supporting a grieving friend or family member. Some of the ideas teach the fundamentals of grief and mourning, while others offer practical day-to-day ways to help. Turn to any page and seize the day by being a real friend in grief today, right now, right this minute.

ISBN 1-879651-26-2
128 pages • Softcover • $11.95
(plus additional shipping and handling)

Companion
PRESS

All Dr. Wolfelt's publications can be ordered by mail from:
Companion Press
3735 Broken Bow Road • Fort Collins, CO 80526
(970) 226-6050 • Fax 1-800-922-6051
www.centerforloss.com

ALSO BY ALAN WOLFELT

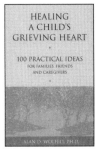

HEALING A CHILD'S GRIEVING HEART: 100 PRACTICAL IDEAS FOR FAMILIES, FRIENDS & CAREGIVERS

An idea book for grown-ups who want practical, day-to-day "how tos" for helping the grieving children they love. Some ideas teach about children's unique mourning styles and needs. Others suggest simple activities and tips for spending time together.

ISBN 1-879651-28-9 • 128 pages • Softcover • $11.95
(plus additional shipping and handling)

HEALING YOUR GRIEVING HEART FOR KIDS: 100 PRACTICAL IDEAS

Simple advice and activities for children after a death. An idea book for young and middle readers (6-12 year-olds) grieving the death of someone loved. The text is simple and straightforward, teaching children about grief and affirming that their thoughts and feelings are not only normal but necessary. Page after page of age-appropriate activities and gentle, healing guidance.

ISBN 1-879651-27-0 • 128 pages • Softcover • $11.95
(plus additional shipping and handling)

Companion
PRESS

All Dr. Wolfelt's publications can be ordered by mail from:
Companion Press
3735 Broken Bow Road • Fort Collins, CO 80526
(970) 226-6050 • Fax 1-800-922-6051
www.centerforloss.com

ALSO BY ALAN WOLFELT

HEALING YOUR GRIEVING HEART FOR TEENS: 100 PRACTICAL IDEAS

Grief is especially difficult during the teen years. This book explains why this is so and offers straightforward, practical advice for healing

ISBN 1-879651-23-8
128 pages • Softcover • $11.95
(plus additional shipping and handling)

HEALING A TEEN'S GRIEVING HEART: 100 PRACTICAL IDEAS FOR FAMILIES, FRIENDS & CAREGIVERS

If you want to help a grieving teen but aren't sure how, this book is for you. It explains the teen's unique mourning needs, offers real-world advice and suggests realistic activities.

ISBN 1-879651-24-6
128 pages • Softcover • $11.95
(plus additional shipping and handling)

Companion
PRESS

All Dr. Wolfelt's publications can be ordered by mail from:
Companion Press
3735 Broken Bow Road • Fort Collins, CO 80526
(970) 226-6050 • Fax 1-800-922-6051
www.centerforloss.com

ALSO BY ALAN WOLFELT

HEALING YOUR TRAUMATIZED HEART: 100 PRACTICAL IDEAS AFTER SOMEONE YOU LOVE DIES A SUDDEN, VIOLENT DEATH

Did you know that more than 43,000 North Americans die in motor vehicle crashes each year? That more than 29,000 complete suicide? That more than 16,000 die from falls? That more than 17,000 die by homicide? Together, more than 150,000 North Americans die each year as a result of sudden, violent death.

Death is never easy, but for families and friends affected by a sudden, violent death, grief is especially traumatic. Deaths caused by accidents, homicide and suicide typically seem premature, unjust, and very, very wrong. Persistent thoughts and feelings about what the death must have been like for the person who died—and what might have been done to prevent it— often color the grief process. Strong feelings of anger and regret are also common. Understanding and expressing these feelings helps survivors, over time and with the support of others, come to reconcile their loss.

ISBN 1-879651-32-7
128 pages • Softcover • $11.95
(plus additional shipping and handling)

Companion
PRESS

All Dr. Wolfelt's publications can be ordered by mail from:
Companion Press
3735 Broken Bow Road • Fort Collins, CO 80526
(970) 226-6050 • Fax 1-800-922-6051
www.centerforloss.com

ALSO BY ALAN WOLFELT

THE HEALING YOUR GRIEVING HEART
JOURNAL FOR TEENS

Teenagers often don't want to talk to adults—or even to their friends—about their struggles. But given the opportunity, many will choose the more private option of writing. Many grieving teens find that journaling helps them sort through their confusing thoughts and feelings.

Yet few journals created just for teens exist and even fewer address the unique needs of the grieving teen. In the Introduction, this unique journal affirms the grieving teen's journey and offers gentle, healing guidance. Then, throughout, the authors provide simple, open-ended questions for the grieving teen to explore.

To encourage free expression, other pages in the journal are blank or simply provide brief, life-affirming quotes from the world's greatest thinkers.

Designed just for grieving teens as a companion to Dr. Wolfelt's bestselling *Healing Your Grieving Heart for Teens: 100 Practical Ideas*, this journal will be a comforting, affirming and healing presence for teens in the weeks, months and years after the death of someone loved.

ISBN 1-879651-33-5
128 pages • Softcover • $11.95
(plus additional shipping and handling)

Companion
PRESS

All Dr. Wolfelt's publications can be ordered by mail from:
Companion Press
3735 Broken Bow Road • Fort Collins, CO 80526
(970) 226-6050 • Fax 1-800-922-6051
www.centerforloss.com